D1392607

Suffering and Singing

John Hindley

Suffering and Singing

Knowing God's Love in the Pain and Despair

John Hindley

www.uniontheology.org

a division of 10 of those.com

First published in Great Britain in 2015

Reprinted 2017

British Library Cataloguing in Publication Data

A record for this book is available from the British Library

ISBN: 978-1-910587-37-9

Designed by Steve Devane

Printed in Denmark by Nørhaven

10Publishing, a division of 10ofthose.com

Unit C, Tomlinson Road, Leyland, PR25 2DY, England

Email: info@10ofthose.com

Website: www.10ofthose.com

Psalm 44

For the director of music. Of the Sons of Korah. A maskil.

¹ We have heard it with our ears, O God;
  our ancestors have told us
what you did in their days,
  in days long ago.
² With your hand you drove out the nations
  and planted our ancestors;
you crushed the peoples
  and made our ancestors flourish.
³ It was not by their sword that they won the land,
  nor did their arm bring them victory;
it was your right hand, your arm,
  and the light of your face, for you loved them.

⁴ You are my King and my God,
  who decrees victories for Jacob.
⁵ Through you we push back our enemies;
  through your name we trample our foes.
⁶ I put no trust in my bow,
  my sword does not bring me victory;
⁷ but you give us victory over our enemies,
  you put our adversaries to shame.
⁸ In God we make our boast all day long,
  and we will praise your name for ever.

⁹ But now you have rejected and humbled us;
  you no longer go out with our armies.
¹⁰ You made us retreat before the enemy,
  and our adversaries have plundered us.
¹¹ You gave us up to be devoured like sheep
  and have scattered us among the nations.
¹² You sold your people for a pittance,
  gaining nothing from their sale.

[13] You have made us a reproach to our neighbours,
   the scorn and derision of those around us.
[14] You have made us a byword among the nations;
   the peoples shake their heads at us.
[15] I live in disgrace all day long,
   and my face is covered with shame
[16] at the taunts of those who reproach and revile me,
   because of the enemy, who is bent on revenge.

[17] All this came upon us,
   though we had not forgotten you;
   we had not been false to your covenant.
[18] Our hearts had not turned back;
   our feet had not strayed from your path.
[19] But you crushed us and made us a haunt for jackals;
   you covered us over with deep darkness.

[20] If we had forgotten the name of our God
   or spread out our hands to a foreign god,
[21] would not God have discovered it,
   since he knows the secrets of the heart?
[22] Yet for your sake we face death all day long;
   we are considered as sheep to be slaughtered.

[23] Awake, Lord! Why do you sleep?
   Rouse yourself! Do not reject us for ever.
[24] Why do you hide your face
   and forget our misery and oppression?

[25] We are brought down to the dust;
   our bodies cling to the ground.
[26] Rise up and help us;
   rescue us because of your unfailing love.

CONTENTS

For those who are hurting

I assume that your heart is broken and that you are tired with pain. You may well have no tears left for your sobs and be lurching between fear and anger. There are few good marriages, and most singleness is terribly lonely. Bringing up children is hard, and not bringing up children is hard. No-one lives that long without grieving someone close to them, and those wounds do not close. Illness lays us low and cancer scares us. I am not yet forty and I have buried friends from this disease. One friend is going through chemotherapy at the moment, while today – as I write this – another friend is having a scan to see if the hints a doctor picked up are cancer. Eighteen months ago I sat in the same waiting room, though it turned out the lump was nothing to worry about. Then there is the simple suffering of life – work pressures, household chores, money worries and debts, difficult friendships and family tensions. Life is often a grind.

Of course there is joy, hope and laughter, and my life has been far freer from suffering than many I know. I almost feel embarrassed to write about this subject – what do I have to say? But we must look suffering in the face and square up to it, and not hide, run or escape from it. The latter are all the options the world around has to offer us – we could escape the pain of life in a beer can, a cult TV series, a shopping spree or an idyllic holiday. Or we could pretend that life is good, and update our status with a smiley face.

we must look suffering in the face and square up to it, and not hide, run or escape from it

We do not struggle with the laughter and joy, and we do not struggle to know where God is in these. We talk of how the Lord has blessed us with a new job or how grateful we are that we can go on holiday. We are slower to see the blessing in redundancy or be grateful for the cancelled holiday as we drive to the hospital.

In this book we are going to see how the pain of suffering nearly overwhelms the faith of God's people. We will see how it threatens to break their trust in a God they have known and experienced and been close to for years. We are going to see that the writers of this psalm are faithful men who have served the Lord well and feel utterly confused by the way he is letting them suffer. And then we will see how he draws them to himself through their suffering – how he turns it from being a mark of his distance from them to an experience of his closeness to them. We will also see how God displays his love for us and his approval of us through our sufferings.

This book simply follows Psalm 44. It is a hard psalm, because it faces up to the truth of suffering. Yet since it is a hard psalm, it is also a glorious one, because the hope and love that it holds out are solid. They are as solid as a cross and as glorious as an empty tomb.

Wherever you are as you read this, I pray that you will see, know and feel the love of Christ in and through your suffering. I am confident that God will answer this prayer for you, for he is a Father who gives good things to his children.

The suffering singers

Perhaps they looked at their instruments stacked against walls, avoiding one another's eyes. What do you do when your heart is broken, when your soul is shrivelled and dying of thirst? What do you sing when the news is of the slain, the defeats and the shame of God's people?

What do *you* do when you are ground down by suffering, when your hopes are dashed, your body is aching and sleep elusive? What do you do when the boss says how sorry he is, but they need to let people go? What do you do when the doctor gently tells you that she thinks this pain is cancer? What do you do when another pregnancy ends in death and despair? What do you do when you stand by the grave three years later and it is just more painful, more confusing? What do you do as another friend, but not you, gets married? What do you do when there is just so little joy and lightness in your life, and the daily routine is grinding you down? What do you do when the darkness will not lift? I do not know what you are suffering, but God does, and he guides these words for you as I write them. He knows suffering, and he knows yours.

The sons of Korah knew suffering. It was underlined in their name. Korah was not their dad (he was a distant ancestor) but they were named for him because he was famous – notorious. He was the cousin of Moses and Aaron (Exodus 6:18–24), which made his rebellion against their God-given authority all the worse. In Numbers 16 he demanded an equal share in the leadership of God's people, and he was judged by God with decisive speed. The Lord caused the ground to open and Korah and all his family went down to their graves alive.

But in Numbers 26:11 Moses wrote simply: 'The line of Korah, however, did not die out.' Whether they were spared or brought back from the grave by the Lord we are not told, but they are the ones who lived when they should have died. They were redeemed from death. They are like us Christians, who should have died and yet live through the wonder and power of the resurrection of Jesus Christ.

Their history, their title as sons of Korah, was a mark of shame and suffering and of the forgiveness and love of the Lord. They knew the suffering of God's judgment and they knew the wonder of his grace.

They also knew the heights, the glory days of Israel. They were chosen by David, the great king of Israel, the slayer of the giant Goliath, and a man after God's own heart. They were appointed to be the singers (1 Chronicles 25:1-8; Heman was a descendent of Korah, as we see from the title of Psalm 88) and gatekeepers (1 Chronicles 26:1) in the temple of God. If you are a Christian, you share their privilege. Chosen by God to follow his Son, to be filled with his Spirit and to herald his good news, you know, or have known, the glory days.

The sons of Korah knew God and they knew suffering; both ran through their family history like threads. But suffering was not only a family trait; it was a present reality for them. The suffering they will go on to describe in Psalm 44 is terrible. They are ashamed, scared, scattered and facing death. These are no super-spiritual saints; they are people who know the grinding and crushing confusion and pain of ongoing suffering. If life is hard for you, they get that, and sing their song alongside you.

We are going to focus on Psalm 44 in this book. We need to begin by placing it in the flow of the Psalms. There are five books of these songs, and the second book begins, in Psalms 42–49, with a sequence of psalms of the sons of Korah. The first book was written by David, so it is appropriate that the second starts with a series by the singers he appointed. Yet the songs of the sons of Korah open with three songs of crushing pain.

Psalm 42 pictures a deer panting for water. This is no cute, soft-focus image, rather it is a picture of frantic desperation. The soul of these singers is on the verge of death, panting for want of God. In the midst of suffering their memories of the glorious days of festivals and feasts at the temple seem like bitter taunts. They are cast down and in turmoil as they compare their current pain with the days when they worshipped God and led his people in praise and thanksgiving. The psalm finishes in hope, a confident expectation that 'I will yet praise him, my Saviour and my God' (42: 11). It finishes with hope, but with no end to the suffering.

Psalm 43 finishes with the same hope – phrased exactly the same way. It has no title, but the repeat of the chorus (43:5), which is identical to that in Psalm 42:5 and 11, makes it clear that the sons of Korah wrote this psalm. It picks up the worst pain of suffering, deeper even than the suffering itself – the pain of feeling that God has rejected you.

Psalms 42 and 43 end in hope, but there is no answer, no resolution. They leave us with the pain of suffering, and with the deepest problem of faith: God is in charge, Christ is Lord and so when terrible suffering comes we cannot pretend it has nothing to do with him. We must either run from him – shaking our fist in bitter agony, and hating the Jesus who brought

God is in charge, Christ is Lord and so when terrible suffering comes we cannot pretend it has nothing to do with him

such evil and hurt into our lives, homes, families and hearts – or we must run to him in hope, trust, faith and love. Psalm 44 shows us how we can do this, why we must do this and how Christ himself will hedge us in like a scrum of bodyguards as we flee to refuge in him.

But it is not an easy thing to do. When I meet people who have turned from Jesus because of their suffering or that which they see around them, and who now hate him and deny him and insult him, I think they have grasped something incredibly important. They have seen that Jesus' power and authority are even over suffering. He could prevent it. This is the truth we would rather duck, but cannot. Atheists and Christians have the same question: 'How can a good God allow such misery, cruelty, pain and suffering that simply is not our fault?' We will see, as we work through this psalm, that the answer, at first hard and then beautifully glorious, is that suffering is a season God brings us into in love, and for our blessing. I know you might find that hard to stomach now and I pray that you will smile through the tears as you read on. If you can, why not take a few minutes now to pray that the psalm might be Christ's way of loving you in the middle of your suffering?

You see, in their confusion and agony of suffering the sons of Korah caught each other's eye, clutched their instruments, struck a chord and sang. They sang with tears, but they sang to God. And the Holy Spirit gave them words to lead our heavy hearts back to Jesus along with theirs. They raise this most sickening of questions – how can God allow our suffering? – and they answer it.

Notice how the title of Psalm 44 tells us that they answer it in a song: 'For the director of music. Of the Sons of Korah. A maskil.' Jesus, our great worship leader, our director of music, leads us in singing it too. It is a psalm that does not shy away from the reality, confusion, shame and terror of suffering. And it is a psalm that takes us to Jesus. Because of the love of Christ for us, we can learn to turn to him, to sing to him and to pray to him, whatever may come. That is why the Holy Spirit wrote Psalm 44 for us.

God has always helped his people

3

PSALM 44:1–3

Psalm 44 starts strangely for a psalm dealing with suffering. Where Psalm 42 starts with pain and desperation, Psalm 44 starts with blessing. This is not a psalm wrung out of midnight wakefulness, beginning in pain and need. It is raw, but it is also considered, and that makes it all the more important, and even risky. It is a psalm that wants to set our pain squarely in the context of God's faithfulness.

In verse 1 the temple singers look back to their childhood: 'We have heard it with our ears, O God; our ancestors have told us what you did in their days, in days long ago.' Their nation has a long history of God coming to their aid. Verse 2 continues, 'With your hand you drove out the nations and planted our ancestors; you crushed the peoples and made our ancestors flourish.' As they write this they take in the sweep of history from God freeing his people from slavery and oppression in Egypt to him giving them the Promised Land, driving out the wicked nations who lived there and leading his people in.

They are reminding themselves – and us – that the love of God for his people was never just a nice idea, or merely a deep affection of God's heart, but was also worked out in practice. God loved his people and so he freed them, protected them, led them and provided for them. God's love is the care of a husband and the compassion of a father, not the fickle feeling of a romantic teenager. This is how God loves us, how he loves you. It does raise hard questions about why he is letting you suffer as you are, but it also gives us hope. The very truths that make faith hard also make faith beautiful. That is the tension we feel when we suffer – we don't know what Christ is doing, and yet we want Christ close in his love.

God's love is the care of a husband and the compassion of a father

In verse 3 the sons of Korah emphasise that the history of their people is one of complete dependence: 'It was not by their sword that they won the land, nor did their arm bring them victory; it was your right hand, your arm, and the light of your face, for you loved them.' They owed everything to God. They were not partners with him, shouldering the burden and fighting the battles as equals. No, they were children: rescued, carried, loved and cared for by their God.

This love that God had for them was shown in action – he did for them what they could not do for themselves. But it was also shown in relationship. He delighted in them and so showed them the light of his face. This recalls the long hours Moses would sit face to face with the Lord until his face shone in reflection of the light in God's face (Exodus 33:7–11; 34:29–35).

There are two reasons why Psalm 44 starts with blessing, when its goal is to confront suffering. The first is that the writers' knowledge of the history of God's love for his people makes the present misery of Israel all the more painful and confusing for them, as we will see. The second is that it draws them to bring their suffering to God, and to search for his love in the pits of life as well as on the heights.

We have even more reason to recount the love of God than they did. We share their history, those of us who follow Christ, whether we are descendants of Abraham or Gentiles graciously brought into Israel (Galatians 3:7–9). And we have an even greater, more recent, history. The love of Christ for us was displayed as he died our death on the cross. The price of our freedom from death, sin, judgment, guilt and shame was the blood of Christ poured out as he hung cursed on the cross, cut off from his Father in our place and going through the hell we deserved to free us from God's judgment and wrath. This is the love that our God has for us. You have seen the light of his love for you in his thorn-crowned face.

> *The love of Christ for us was displayed as he died our death on the cross*

We know that everything we have is the gift of God. We brought no goodness or righteousness to him so that he would forgive us. No, we sinned and he suffered. We did evil and he died. Yet through Jesus we are forgiven, free, loved and adopted as children of God. The history of God with his people is wonderful, glorious and true. It is the history of a God who loves and loves, who pours himself out for our sake. It is the story of Jesus who went through hell to find you and bring you back to himself.

Add to this the ways our Father has cared for you and your church over the years. How has he whispered his love for you personally? How has he led and guided your church when all seemed hopeless?

If you are suffering greatly now, then to hold this vision of the past goodness of God alongside your current pain probably results in a mixture of deep reassurance and painful confusion. It is good to know that God has loved us, and still loves us, but why is he letting *this* happen now? Has his love changed? Does he really still love me? Is he angry? Or has he simply grown cold? Maybe I have grown cold and that is why I cannot see the light of his face now?

The sons of Korah want us to plumb the depths of our confusion and hurt, and they are going to take us further down still. But we will come up as the psalm draws towards its close. They want us to plumb the depths with them so that we will find, with them, that there is no depth where God will not find us, no darkness where his light cannot shine. There is no distance Jesus will not travel to take us in his arms, lift us onto his shoulders and bring us home into pleasant pastures beside still waters.

Our trust is in God

PSALM 44:4–8

4

The sons of Korah know how their Lord has been faithful in the past and this is not simple nostalgia for them; it is theology. In verses 4–8 they sing to God their conclusions from their knowledge of the scriptures – they sing their trust and their hope.

In verse 4 they declare, 'You are my King and my God, who decrees victories for Jacob.' The idea behind the 'victories' here is not simply triumph but deliverance or salvation. They likely have in mind victories like the one the Lord won over Pharaoh's army in the Red Sea that decisively freed his people from slavery in Egypt. In this verse they express the fact and nature of the rule of our God.

Our God is a king – Jesus is the Christ, the one

anointed by the Spirit to be the eternal king over God's people. His rule is not only based on the fact that he created all things (although that would be enough reason!) but also on his Father appointing him as the firstborn from the dead so that he might be supreme over all things (Colossians 1:15–18).

Our God is a king, a warrior king and a servant king, and the nature of his kingship is to rescue, save and serve his people. He is not a king seeking to lord it over those he rules, as other kings might. He is a king who sweeps into battle to save his people. He sweeps into battle to save you. His victories are not won to merely prove his might; they are won as an outworking of his love for those he rules. When Christ rode into battle against sin and death on the cross, he wept for you, he bled for you and he was willing to die for he loves you.

He is a king who sweeps into battle to save his people. He sweeps into battle to save you

The sons of Korah were happy to enter into battle against their enemies, following such a king. They were confident that he would lead them into victory: 'Through you we push back our enemies; through your name we trample our foes' (Psalm 44:5). Like them, we are right to have confidence in Christ that we can fight alongside him against even the most terrible enemies. In Romans 16:20, Paul reassures his readers that, 'The God of peace will soon crush Satan under your feet.' Having crushed the head of Satan on the cross, Jesus now gives us his Spirit that we might do the same.

This might sound strange – how can Satan have *been* crushed by Jesus and yet will *soon be* crushed under our feet? It is like being an Israelite warrior in the valley of Elah (1 Samuel 17). They held their breath as a boy, David, strode towards the giant Goliath, heard David's confident trust in the Lord and caught a blur as his stone flew. Then they blinked twice as the colossal champion fell. Next, they didn't even think – the enemy were running and their arms punched their spears in the air as they shouted the war cry of Israel. The priests blew the horns, and David and Saul led the army in a chaotic charge at the Philistine lines. The rout was long as they pursued the enemies of God as far as Gath. So we will crush Satan – as one already slain by Christ. The battles of suffering that we face against despair, fear and crushing anxiety are spiritual, and we fight with the sword of the Spirit, armoured with the salvation Christ has supplied (Ephesians 6:10–20). We face enemies that should terrify us, and that do terrify us, but they are enemies already slain by Christ, already broken, and defeated.

So does that mean that *our* seeming defeat in the battle, which seems to happen all too often, is down to our failure to fight well? When the darkness of suffering's gloom overwhelms us, is it because our hands have grown weak, the sword has slipped and we are not keeping the shield of faith up against the onslaught? It would give God an easy way out for us to blame our sufferings on our sin, but this is not where the sons of Korah turn. Having affirmed that we do indeed fight alongside our heavenly king with the weapons he supplies, they hammer home their point that this does not make victory or defeat reliant on us: 'I do not trust in my bow, my sword does not bring me victory; but you give us victory over our enemies, you put our adversaries to shame' (Psalm 44:6–7).

We fight because the battle has already been won. We can trample Satan underfoot because Jesus has already triumphed over him by the cross. By the grace of God we fight, but we fight a battle where he has already killed the giant. Not only that, but we fight with the promise that Jesus will bring all his soldiers home safe to his Father's side, for we are 'more than conquerors' through Christ (Romans 8:37).

It is this confidence in God that brings the sons of Korah to the end of the first part of their psalm with the confession that, 'In God we make our boast all day long, and we will praise your name for ever' (Psalm 44:8). They *do* make their boast in God and they *will* continue to praise him. This is an expression of their current faith in God and their expectation that they will continue to have this faith.

> *We boast in Christ, and especially in his cross (Galatians 6:14)*

God is their boast, and they are right to make him so. Nothing has changed since they first sang this song.

We boast in Christ, and especially in his cross (Galatians 6:14). It is on the cross that Jesus displayed the depths of his love for his people. It is on the same cross that he won the decisive and ultimate victory, defeating Satan and rescuing us from his power and plans. This is why Paul twice commands the Corinthians, 'Let the one who boasts boast in the Lord' (1 Corinthians 1:31 and 2 Corinthians 10:17).

The sons of Korah have spent eight verses affirming their trust in God, expressing their complete dependence on God and declaring their praise of God. God is the rock we run to in suffering, and they have given us good reason to do so.

But maybe God doesn't feel to you like a rock of refuge in your suffering? Perhaps Christ feels more like a stone – deaf to your cries. Or maybe you even feel like it is his hand that is holding you down, that he is crushing you with suffering. Just yesterday I felt burdened by work, my sin, exhausting hurts and problems in the lives of friends in my church, and nothing seemed to go right. I felt that Christ was loading burdens onto me rather than taking them from me. Even in my low-level suffering, the cross of Christ did not seem to connect with my day. If Jesus has won such a victory for me, why is my life so hard? Do you feel like that? And for deeper and more painful reasons than mine?

If you do, you are not alone. The sons of Korah have begun with faith, praise and deep dependence on their God both because this is truly how they feel and also because this is what makes the 'But …' at the start of verse 9 so horrific. Psalm 44 captures the bizarre confusion of suffering that goes alongside the horror and pain of it so powerfully because it sets suffering in the context of faith. We can see why murderous Egypt suffered the judgment of God, but why would faithful Israel? Why would God bring such suffering on them? Why would God bring such suffering on you?

We can see why murderous Egypt suffered the judgment of God, but why would faithful Israel?

As the sons of Korah phrase it, 'In God we make our boast all day long, and we will praise your name for ever. Selah. But …'

But God has slaughtered us

5

PSALM 44:9–16

'But now you have rejected and humbled us …' (verse 9). God is everything to the sons of Korah: their boast and the object of their praise; their king and the source of their salvation. However, their God, in whom they have placed all their trust and hope, has humbled and rejected them. The nature of their suffering is hard enough, as we will see – defeat, exile and scorn – but worse than all this is their rejection by God.

In no sense do I want to underestimate the sufferings of those who do not follow Christ, and I do not know how people endure living in this painful world without Christ. The Lord is surely working in the suffering of those who don't follow him, but that is beyond the scope of this book. Terrible though all suffering is, there is a particular edge to suffering that we feel as

Christians. We feel its keenness when we too cry out, 'you have rejected us'. To put your trust in God, fall into suffering and be met with the silence of heaven crushes your soul and breaks your heart. You may well know this pain.

Now, this is a serious accusation to throw at God, but it is not one that the sons of Korah make lightly. The suffering they face is that serious. They are seeing defeat in battle: 'You made us retreat before the enemy, and our adversaries have plundered us' (verse 10). This is hard enough to bear, but it is no minor skirmish or distant campaign. This is a battle for the very survival of God's people that they have lost: 'You gave us up to be devoured like sheep and have scattered us among the nations. You sold your people for a pittance, gaining nothing from their sale' (verses 11–12).

'You gave us up to be devoured like sheep and have scattered us among the nations...'

The people are not merely defeated; they are devoured. They are dead or destroyed, and all the survivors are exiled from their land. We are not told which exile this refers to, but that is not the point. The point is that this is a national catastrophe. There would have been untold misery rolled into these lines from the song. Soldiers lying dead on the battlefield was just the start, soon followed by the tears of wives and mothers. We cannot imagine how these became screams as the victorious enemy began to take the young off to the slave caravans. Families were surely left grieving, split apart, plundered and starving. If we saw these images on the TV news, we would be moved and shocked.

The psalm spares us the details, but the language evokes the scale of this tragedy – 'devoured', 'scattered' and 'sold'. God has sold his people into slavery. They are destroyed. And then insult is added to injury: 'You have made us a reproach to our neighbours, the scorn and derision of those around us. You have made us a byword among the nations; the peoples shake their heads at us' (verses 13–14). As well as being destroyed, they are laughed at. The nations around are glad to see the shame of Israel. This people claimed such love and protection from their God, but 'Where is he now?' they no doubt laugh. Every vile sin and callous misery is inflicted on

God's chosen people and he does nothing. So the sons of Korah bring the conclusive evidence to back up their chilling accusation: 'you have rejected us'.

This is a national disaster, and also a deeply shocking attack on the faith of the sons of Korah. What does this defeat mean for the promises God made to Abraham (first expressed in Genesis 12:1–3)? How can the Lord now bless all nations through Abraham's family if that family is slaughtered and scattered? To face rejection by God would be terrible for any nation, but for Israel it seems like God is rejecting his own promises along with them; it seems that he is rejecting humanity and leaving us without hope.

Israel faces a national disaster that strikes at the core of God's faithfulness and love. This is also a personal agony for our psalm-writers. In verses 15 and 16 they move from referring to 'we' or 'us' to 'I' or 'me': 'I live in disgrace all day long, and my face is covered with shame at the taunts of those who reproach and revile me, because of the enemy, who is bent on revenge.'

They are not writing this psalm at a distance. They are not safe in some hidden fortress feeling the disgrace of their people second-hand. No, this is personal pain: '*my* face is covered with shame'. They hear the taunts and they wipe the spit from their faces. They cry themselves sick and hurt more deeply than they knew they could.

And the terrible truth is that the Lord is behind this. Their praise and trust, their love and faith in God is what makes the suffering so very hard. In the depths of the night, when we lose hold of all else, we cry out, 'Why do you *allow* this, Lord?' And then perhaps we whisper, 'Why do you *do* this, Lord?'

The suffering of the sons of Korah is a picture, an echo, of the suffering of the Son of God

In asking these questions we open up a terrible possibility that our faith is misplaced, but we, and the sons of Korah, echo the cry of God himself. At the bottom depths of the darkest pit of suffering the cosmos will ever know, the Son of God cried out, 'My God, my God, why have your forsaken me?' (Matthew 27:46). The suffering of the sons of Korah is a picture, an echo, of the suffering of the Son of God. The rejection of Israel,

God's adopted son (Hosea 11:1), seems impossible to understand, so how much more incomprehensible is the rejection of Jesus, God's eternal Son? When you cry out asking why the Lord has rejected you, you are echoing the cry of the greatest man of faith to have ever lived. You stand with your Saviour, and that is a good place to stand.

Psalm 44 throws us on the cross of Christ. It prises open the sufferings he faced there. It begins to unlock our hearts to what he suffered in our place, what he endured for us. As you suffer, you begin to feel something of what Christ felt; your heart begins to beat along with his. This is where we begin to see why the Lord might give such suffering to his people, to you his child. It is a door to seeing his love for us. This is where the sons of Korah are taking us. They will frame our suffering, along with theirs, with the rough wood of a Roman cross. In that frame, the picture will begin to make sense. But

This is where the sons of Korah are taking us. They will frame our suffering, along with theirs

we must not rush ahead, because the cross of Christ raises questions as well as answering them.

If Christ is rejected for us, if he suffers in our place, if he is indeed our sacrifice and substitute – bringing us forgiveness, love, adoption, life, grace, joy and hope at the cost of his blood – then why do we suffer? If he suffered in our place, then surely we need not suffer at all? And, more pointedly, if he was rejected by God so that we (though we well deserve it) will never be rejected, then why does God reject the sons of Korah in their suffering? Why does he reject you and me?

We will come to see how God gently and remarkably addresses these devastating concerns we have. Before we do so, there is one more nail that the sons of Korah have had driven into their flesh. This suffering is not only terrible, it is also undeserved.

And we do not deserve it

6

PSALM 44:17–21

I usually write in the central library in Norwich. On my way here this morning, I walked along by the river past a beautiful carved seat that has been there for a few months now. It is in memory of a man, or boy – I only read his name and a beautiful inscription about pulling in the catch together. I walked past the fishermen setting up for the day as well. I don't know if this lovely memorial was set up by a father whose son is gone, or by grandchildren at their grandpa's favourite fishing spot, or even by buddies for their friend. Most times when I walk past it, my eyes well up a little, because it speaks simply of the pain of grief that ends happy days spent together on the river. I think it is a solid statement of goodness lost in the middle of the confusion and pain of grief.

The confusion of grief and of all suffering is very real. If you are suffering at the moment, you may find it hard to express your pain and fears. You may well feel confused and unsure, making it hard to find the words. It is one of the reasons why Christ gave us the psalms, to give us his words to describe our pain.

If you are a Christian, then this might well make your suffering seem all the more confusing. See if you resonate with what the sons of Korah felt so painfully:

All this came upon us, though we had not forgotten you; we had not been false to your covenant. Our hearts had not turned back; our feet had not strayed from your path. But you crushed us and made us a haunt for jackals; you covered us over with deep darkness. If we had forgotten the name of our God or spread out our hands to a foreign god, would not God have discovered it, since he knows the secrets of the heart? (verses 17–21).

God had brought suffering on them, and they did not deserve it. They have clearly been considering whether they could deserve it for their sins, and we should too. Could it be that the suffering you face, or that those around you face, is as a result of your sin? The answer is that it could be, but if so you will know that this is the case. If, for example, you have been stealing money at work, and are suffering fear because you have been found out and you're waiting to be fired and probably taken to court, then there is a clear link between your sin and your suffering.

If you can see that your suffering is caused by your sin, then there is a wonderfully simple solution – turn to Christ in repentance and faith. Your sin has been paid for on the cross, Christ has forgiven you, and it does not define you. As you stand before God, you do so with the righteousness of Christ. So you can do the same before your employer – confess your sin, the full extent of it, and apologise. Repay if you are able to do so, or make provision to do so in the future. Tell the police everything and make their job easy. Know that whether the future holds prison or freedom, Christ is Lord over it, and he will plot the course of your life; your sin does not hold that power. You are no longer a slave to sin, but a slave to Christ. Whether you have stolen or sinned in another way, that does not define and control you; Jesus does.

We need to be so careful with this, though. Even if there is a clear link between your behaviour and suffering, it does not mean that your behaviour was necessarily sinful. There are plenty of causes of suffering that have nothing to do with sin. You may have a bad back from working for years as a builder; sore and damaged knees because you enjoy jogging; or potential health issues because you enjoy alcohol in moderation. There is nothing inherently sinful about building, jogging or beer, wine and whisky. These activities can be sinful – you can build a tower in Babel, you can run because freedom lies there (not in Christ) and you can drink because that is your joy and god. But it simply does not work that dishonest, cowboy builders get bad backs and honest, hard-working ones don't. Suffering can follow sin, but it doesn't have to.

So how do you know whether your sin has caused your suffering? I think you usually do. Others may not, but you will probably have a sense of it, though you may be embarrassed to tell people if this is the case. Last week I woke up one day with a headache, and blamed it on a busy time and tiredness. I knew that the whisky before bed had been unwise, but didn't want to admit it. If you are really not sure, though, then pray and ask your Father to show you whether your sin is the reason.

If he shows you that your sin has caused your suffering, then confess your sin to him and repent, turn back to him and learn by heart the promise in 1 John 1:9: 'If we confess our sins, he is faithful and just and will forgive us our sins and purify us from all unrighteousness.' This is important, because confessing and repenting might not end the suffering, but this doesn't mean you are unforgiven.

I know Christians who have made themselves miserable by assuming that ongoing suffering in their lives is a result of sin. They root around and quarry the depths of their souls to seek out and confess the tiniest sin and so end their suffering. But they, and you, are forgiven. When Christ said on the cross, 'It is finished' (John 19:30), he meant that he had paid the full price for all your

I know Christians who have made themselves miserable by assuming that ongoing suffering in their lives is a result of sin

sin. When he sat down at the right hand of his Father (Hebrews 10:12), it was because his work of saving us was complete.

Christ died to take the anger of God at sin; he experienced our guilt and our shame in our place so that we would not

Of course your suffering may have nothing to do with your sin at all. Yet whether that is true or whether your suffering was caused by sin you have now confessed, it is no longer caused by your sin. Christ died to take the anger of God at our sin; he experienced our guilt and our shame in our place so that we would not. There are no nails, no cries, no gasps, no wounds and no despair left for you to suffer for your sins. Jesus paid it all.

So why then do we suffer? If Christ suffered for us, why do we hurt so much? You can hear the confusion in the voices of the sons of Korah: 'Our hearts had not turned back' (verse 18). And we know this confusion. It makes us run from suffering. We run to any distraction from the pain – food, drink, constant busyness, spending money or earning praise. We run, or we sink, consumed by the darkness. We run or we sink because we feel we cannot run to God, since he is behind the pain and he should be the one behind the joy.

The impulse to run is right, but we so often run the wrong way. We should run to the Rock, to our Refuge and Shield: Jesus. He is the one who helps us in our time of need (Hebrews 4:16). When we are confused by suffering because we know it is both undeserved and from God, then we stand in good company. As he hung on the cross, Christ was spotlessly innocent: 'He committed no sin, and no deceit was found in his mouth' (1 Peter 2:22). He was innocent and he was suffering at God's hand, crying out to the seemingly oblivious heavens, 'My God, my God, why have you forsaken me?' (Matthew 27:46).

When we suffer but have not sinned, we know that the one who sits on the throne of heaven alongside his Father knows exactly what we feel in all its agony and perplexity. And that is where this psalm, and all our suffering, will come to a climax.

Yet it is for God's sake

7

PSALM 44:22 AND ROMANS 8:31-39

'Yet for your sake we face death all day long; we are considered as sheep to be slaughtered' (verse 22). The 'yet' at the beginning of verse 22 is like a handbrake turn that dramatically changes the direction of the psalm. This terrible suffering of the sons of Korah, which feels like death and slaughter, is for God's sake.

The resolution does not come from seeing how the suffering is from God – that is, by debating to what extent he causes it, or whether he simply allows the suffering of a fallen world and sinful humanity to strike us. The resolution does not come from seeing whether our sin has played a part in our suffering. The resolution does not come from seeing how our suffering might be a means to discipline us and refine us to greater holiness. These are all important questions, worth exploring. But they cannot be the first questions. We can only begin to ask and answer them once we have seen something more important than the origins or ends of our suffering.

The scope of this psalm, and this book, is to set up the horrendous pain of suffering and then to give us one answer which cuts to the heart of our confusion and fear. It is simply this: God has sent our suffering for his sake. We do not suffer primarily because we may have sinned; we suffer because we are his. Suffering is not a mark of God's indifference towards us, or his hatred of us. Suffering is a mark of his love for us. It shows that we are *his*.

> *We do not suffer primarily because we may have sinned; we suffer because we are his*

This is the flow of the psalm. After they have so eloquently and agonisingly laid their suffering bare, and so simply declared their innocence in the face of it, the sons of Korah tell us that the suffering is for God's sake. They are not suffering for the sake of their sin; they are suffering for the sake of their God. Their suffering shows that they are God's people. It shows the world that they are loved by the Lord of lords and King of kings.

This seems utterly perverse, crooked and wrong to us. Surely wealth, comfort, good health and peace are the marks of those loved by God? If such a mighty God loves you, won't he hedge you in and protect you from anything that could harm you? That is the logic of our world, and it makes such clear sense to us. It is why suffering is so confusing – 'I love God, and he should protect me, shouldn't he? And aren't there Bible verses that back this up?'

But what if that was not how God showed his love? What if the heart of the Bible and the cosmos was about the love of God being shown in bringing suffering on the one he loves most dearly? What if the love of God is shown more clearly on a cross than a throne? What if he prepares a feast for you *after* he has brought you through the valley of the shadow of death?

> We all, like sheep, have gone astray, each of us has turned to our own way; and the LORD has laid on him the iniquity of us all.

He was oppressed and afflicted, yet he did not open his mouth; he was led like a lamb to the slaughter, and as a sheep before its shearers is silent, so he did not open his mouth. By oppression and judgment he was taken away. Yet who of his generation protested? For he was cut off from the land of the living; for the transgression of my people he was punished. He was assigned a grave with the wicked, and with the rich in his death, though he had done no violence, nor was any deceit in his mouth. Yet it was the LORD's will to crush him and cause him to suffer, and though the LORD makes his life an offering for sin, he will see his offspring and prolong his days, and the will of the LORD will prosper in his hand (Isaiah 53:6–10).

Jesus was slaughtered like a sheep and it was the Lord's will to crush him. We too are considered sheep to be slaughtered. What Psalm 44:22 is teaching us is that when we are suffering at the hand of the Lord,

We too are considered sheep to be slaughtered

our Father is treating us like Jesus, his Son. Suffering is a mark of God's love. If you suffer as a Christian, it is not because God is powerless, any more than he was powerless to end the sufferings of Christ. If you are a Christian and you suffer, it is because God loves you.

This is the path that our Father leads his children along. When Paul writes of us being children of God, this is what he concludes: 'The Spirit himself testifies with our spirit that we are God's children. Now if we are children, then we are heirs – heirs of God and co-heirs with Christ, if indeed we share in his sufferings in order that we may also share in his glory' (Romans 8:16–17). We are heirs of God alongside Jesus. We share the same relationship with our Father that his only begotten Son enjoys. As a natural outworking of that love, our Father treats us like his Son. We share in his sufferings in order to share in his glory.

There are different ways that the Father uses suffering to bring us to share in Christ's glory. He uses it to discipline us, to refine us and to show us how precious his love is – more precious than whatever we lose through the suffering. He may do this by taking away things that tempt us to worship them instead of him, or he may simply bring suffering to grow us in our dependence on his love or our compassion towards others. He wounds us to draw us back to himself (Hosea 6:1), and he sometimes does this as we only just begin to wander.

He also leads us through a valley darkened by the very shadow of death, not because we are wandering but so that we will see more truly that there is no light but Christ. The path to Christ's glory is the path of the cross. There is no other way. The wonder of following Jesus is that we can 'Consider it pure joy, my brothers and sisters, whenever you face trials of many kinds …' (James 1:2), because the testing of our faith proves and increases its strength.

The path to Christ's glory is the path of the cross. There is no other way

This world was not made for death and futility, but as a result of Adam's sin God has given it over to just that (Romans 8:18–21; see also 1:18–32). And to be a child of God is to experience the world like Jesus did. We can ask questions in our suffering and see why the Lord has brought this particular pain on us, and the sons of Korah will go on to cry out like this. But the one thing we need to know is that we do not suffer aimlessly, or at the hands of an indifferent deity. We suffer for the Lord's sake. We are slaughtered like sheep, in a similar way to how the Son was as the Lamb of God. He died for our sin, suffering hell in our place; we will never suffer like that, we will never be cut off from God as he was, but the pattern is the same. He suffered and then entered his glory. We will suffer and then enter his glory.

This is not easy to take hold of, and we need to stop and pray for the Spirit's wisdom and the eyes of faith. But the terrible pain of your present, ongoing and suffocating suffering is a mark that the Father loves you. This is precisely how Paul sees Psalm 44:22:

> Who shall separate us from the love of Christ? Shall trouble or hardship or persecution or famine or nakedness or danger or sword? As it is written: "For your sake we face death all day long; we are considered as sheep to be slaughtered." No, in all these things we are more than conquerors through him who loved us. For I am convinced that neither death nor life, neither angels nor demons, neither the present nor the future, nor any powers, neither height nor depth, nor anything else in

all creation, will be able to separate us from the love of God that is in Christ Jesus our Lord (Romans 8:35–39).

That we suffer for God's sake transforms suffering. Paul is simply showing us that if suffering comes to us as a sign of our Father's love, there is nothing left that can separate us from that love. If we are loved in and through our suffering, just as the Father loved Jesus in and through his suffering, then we are always loved. The world will point at us, as they pointed at Christ, and ask where our God is as we suffer. The answer is that he is with us, behind us and before us, giving us suffering as a mark of his love to bring us to the glory of his Son.

God sees your suffering, he appoints it and he loves you. You suffer for his sake. So how then should you approach your suffering? The sons of Korah cry out to him, and we will too.

So we wait for him to come

8

PSALM 44:23–26

So then, if suffering is a mark of God's love for us, if it is where our Father meets us, sustains us, refines us and draws us to a deeper understanding that we are his children, then should we embrace it? Should we see our pain as a good thing? Wonderfully, we should not. We should revel in the good that the Lord brings out of our hurts and struggles. We should stand in awe of a Father who brings us into the glory of his Son by the same path of suffering that Christ walked. But we do not need to call the suffering itself good.

Suffering cannot overcome us, because we suffer for God's sake. Suffering cannot overcome us, because God shows us his love in it. Suffering cannot overcome us, and so we pray for it to end. Psalm 44 finishes with such a prayer:

Awake, Lord! Why do you sleep? Rouse yourself! Do not reject us for ever. Why do you hide your face and forget our misery and oppression? We are brought down to the dust; our bodies cling to the ground. Rise up and help us; rescue us because of your unfailing love (verses 23–26).

This prayer still expresses the consistent faith of the sons of Korah as they ask the Lord to redeem them '… because of your unfailing love'. But they are still asking for an end to the suffering. Suffering is an expression of the love of God because the table of glorious feasting lies at the end of the way through the valley of the shadow of death. The suffering is a mark of his love, but it is a temporary one.

The suffering is a mark of his love, but it is a temporary one

Our instinctive response to suffering is to ask our heavenly Father to remove or end it. What we have seen in this psalm is that we need to be slower to do so, or at least slower to make this our only prayer. As we cry out to our Father for an end to suffering, we need to see how this particular suffering is a mark of his love for us. He is treating us like Jesus in letting us suffer and he is making us like Jesus by letting us suffer.

As we suffer, we need to look to see and grasp how our Father is loving us through the suffering itself. This will undo the confusion and bitterness of suffering, even if it does not undo the pain. But as we see that suffering means our Father is close to us, and not that he is distant from us, then we do not lean further into suffering. Rather, we lean further into God: 'The name of the LORD is a fortified tower; the righteous run to it and are safe' (Proverbs 18:10). Suffering is a blessing to us because it drives us into the arms of the God whose kind embrace is felt in the pain and whose love is stronger than death. In his arms we pray for his Spirit to fill us, and we pray to know Christ and enjoy him.

And we pray for the suffering to end. Our Father will use suffering, but he will do so to bring us through it into Christ's glory. Suffering is a means, not an end; it's a path, not a destination; it is always temporary. There was no greater agony – physically, emotionally, spiritually and in every other way – than the cross of Christ. And there was no greater defeat of suffering, even death, than the open and empty tomb he left behind on Easter Day.

The Lord will draw his arms around you as you suffer, and he will bring you through suffering to his Son. So ask him to end it. Call on your Christ, as this psalm pictures it, to awake, to rise up and to come to your aid.

In our final chapter we will consider the answer to this prayer, but there is one more issue we need to deal with before we head there. It is that we will be tempted to manipulate this psalm. We live in a world that is terrified of suffering. We spend time, money, insurance and effort on avoiding and minimising suffering and on denying its reality even when we are in the grip of pain and hurt. Living in Britain in the early twenty-first century, I have an incredibly luxurious and comfortable life. Of course, I am aware of the suffering below the surface of my life and the lives of those around me. But that is where I prefer it to stay: below the surface!

We live in a world that is terrified of suffering

So the temptation will be for us to manipulate this psalm, to use it as another technique to avoid suffering. We will easily take the lesson from it that suffering is our Father's way to show his love for us, but once we embrace that, we might reckon that we can then pray for an end to the suffering and God will cause it to end. When we worship comfort, we will happily use God in its service. That will leave us thinking, 'How much do I need to recognise God's love?' Or, 'How many people do I need to piously talk to about the blessing my cancer is before I've done enough for God to answer my prayer for it to end?'

We will all be faced with the temptation to manipulate Christ to bring about a return to comfort, because comfort feels a more tangible and desirable god than Jesus. But to delight in comfort is to so enjoy the departure lounge that we never fly on holiday. The purpose of the good things of this world is to hint at the better – the best – things that lie in the one who created them. So suffer for Christ's sake, and then pray for an end to your sufferings, in order to share in his glory.

He comes to marry us!

9

PSALM 45

Psalm 44 has ended without an answer to the final prayer of the sons of Korah. The answer comes in the next psalm. Psalm 45 is a wedding song; it is the beautiful ballad of the marriage of a king and his bride. Take a moment to read it now. It is hard to imagine a more glorious king:

> You are the most excellent of men and your lips have been anointed with grace, since God has blessed you for ever. Gird your sword on your side, you mighty one; clothe yourself with splendour and majesty. In your majesty ride forth victoriously in the cause of truth, humility and justice; let your right hand achieve awesome deeds. Let your sharp arrows pierce the hearts of the king's enemies; let the nations fall beneath your feet (verses 2–5).

And then the identity of this king, clearly hinted at, is revealed in verse 6: 'Your throne, O God, will last for ever and ever'. The sons of Korah are singing at the wedding feast of God; it is the marriage of God to his bride: to Israel and to the church.

The answer to the prayer that ends Psalm 44 is that Christ will rise up. As suffering surrounds us like wolves in the darkness, we hear a crashing through the trees as our king rides to save us, his torch held high and his sword raised to destroy our foes and fears. Or, more accurately, he rides to us on a donkey, his arms held high to save us as he dies our death, and rises to give himself to us as our life for ever.

The final point of your suffering is that Christ will come to you as a husband who loves you with a burning desire: 'Let the king be enthralled by your beauty' (verse 11). And there are three ways that he will come to you:

1. *Christ comes to you decisively.* If you are not a Christian, then you suffer alone in the darkness, and that is a truly terrible place to be. You need Christ, and he is close to you. He has led you to read this book to draw you to himself. If you were drowning in a storm, it would be a foolish thing to fight off your rescuer as he drags you

into the lifeboat. Christ is for you, he loves you and has died to save you. Now he comes to you in your suffering to take you as his bride. Please, do not reject him.

2. *Christ comes to you repeatedly.* We need Christ to come to us day by day as we struggle in a terrifying world. We have no strength, but he is mighty. We feel bitter and confused, and he brings peace. We are so alone and afraid, and he shows us the depths of his love and hides us in the safety of his Rock. Now he comes to you in your suffering, to sing over you and sustain you. He is Light, Life and anointed with the oil of joy (verse 7), and he is yours.

3. *Christ comes to you finally.* One day the clouds will part and Jesus will come for us. He will come to marry us, to hold us in his arms, to lift our faces to his and to show us his smile of delight over, and welcome for, us. On that day there will be an end to all pain: 'He will wipe every tear from their eyes. There will be no more death or mourning or crying or pain, for the old order of things has passed away' (Revelation 21:4).

Our suffering is terrible, but it is also where our Father shows that we are his children. He shows us, and he shows the world, that he loves us like he loves Jesus as he treats us as he treated Jesus. He will draw us to himself to feel the warmth of that love even as we feel the cold grip of pain and bitter confusion. He will draw us to himself, and make us more like his Son.

Our suffering is terrible, but our suffering will not end in a funeral. It will end in a wedding.

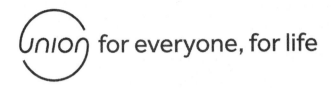 for everyone, for life

If you like what you've read here, check out our website and app. www.uniontheology.org is filled with free, quality resources to bless you.

Our vision is to see the evangelisation of Europe through the raising up of church leaders. To achieve this, our mission under God is to educate and equip pastors, missionaries, church-planters and church-leaders across the continent.

Union offers an affordable, flexible, accessible option for formal theological education.

To find out more, visit:
www.uniontheology.org/courses

 uniontheology.org

@uniontheology

10Publishing is the publishing house of **10ofThose**.

It is committed to producing quality Christian resources that are biblical and accessible.

www.10ofthose.com is our online retail arm selling thousands of quality books at discounted prices. We also service many church bookstalls and can help your church to set up a bookstall. Single and bulk purchases welcome.

For information contact: **sales@10ofthose.com**

or check out our website: **www.10ofthose.com**